THE

Walking
Miracle

BIANCA BREWTON

CONTENTS

Introduction

Testimony

My name is Simone Sahara Brewton. I am 14 years old, and I was diagnosed with Pseudo Obstruction Syndrome at six months of age. The doctors said I probably wouldn't live past a year, but I am still alive. Pseudo Obstruction Syndrome attacks the stomach, small intestines, and large intestines. The news that the doctor gave my parents 14 years ago, was that I would be dependent upon IVs, die, or have a multi-organ transplant.

In order to survive, I have had to be dependent upon IVs (through my chest) for 14 years. For everyone who knows me, that's what I have been hiding in that backpack all those years. I could eat, but no matter what I ate, my stomach would not break down the food.

Please don't feel sad or sorry, just continue to pray for me. One thing that I have truly believed in is that "God really does love me," and as my Grandma Baker always says, "No Weapon Formed Against Simone Will Prosper." The IV access worked until I turned 13. The access was getting harder to find in my chest. With prayers and the guidance of my parents, we made the choice.

We trusted God totally and believed in an MVT which means multiple organs transplant. As I said, "God really loves me. For my Christmas gift, he gave me another lease of life." I received my new organs on December 12, 2007, that include stomach, liver, pancreas, small intestines, and large intestines. I, Simone Sahara Brewton, am asking everyone who reads this story to agree and believe that there will be no rejection in my new organs and no side effects of the medications. I shall live and not die and declare the works of God. (Ps. 118:17)

Much love,

Simone Sahara Brewton.

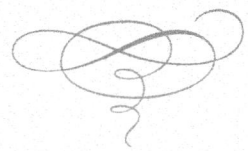

Mom's Journal Entry

May 30, 2008

Luke 9:1-2

"When Jesus had called the Twelve together, he gave them power and authority to drive out all demons, cure diseases, and sent them out to preach the word of the kingdom of God to heal the sick."

Thank you, Jesus, for giving us the power to cure all diseases.

Simone is doing E-X-C-E-L-L-E-N-T. She's just bored. No fever, but still some nausea. These journal updates are getting better. I remember when I had so much to say, and write, on Simone. However, we still need to pray.

I found out today that there is a test called Citrulline that is done twice a week, to see how well her intestines are working.

Well, God showed out again. Dr. Kato told me that Simone's was 30, which is very high, and good. He also said that her intestine function is probably better than his.

Look at God. As cousin Joan always says, "Favor isn't fair."

I also believe Dr. Kato was proud of himself because everything he did for Simone to get another chance in life, worked.

Prayers aren't only working, they are being performed right in front of our eyes. Still working on her kidneys and potassium levels. However, those numbers will come down in a matter of time.

Hugs and Kisses,

Delon and Simone.

Oh yeah! The scope showed no rejection!

THANK YOU, JESUS.

June 1, 2008

Well, Glory to God! Simone is doing WONDERFUL. So wonderful that the doctors have released her on a day pass this Saturday, and Sunday to see family and friends. I told them if they give me one more pass, I am going home for good. On Saturday, she went to visit her Grandmother Baker. She also was able to spend some time with her friends Erica, and Patricia. Girls, thank you for spending time with Simone. You can really tell when kids are being brought up with Godly parents. Even though they haven't had the pleasure of seeing Simone for almost six months, they made her feel welcome. The tube in her nose or the scars on her didn't even phase them. Thank you again. :)

On Sunday, Simone woke up, asking for a pass again. So once again, we went to see grandma, uncle, and auntie. Doesn't she know how much gas costs? (LOL!). She knows her mother would do anything in this world for her. If you could only see Simone when she goes to Grandma's house. The first thing she does is take off her shoes, and the rest is history.

The talk is that tomorrow she might go home. I am still working on her labs. Her potassium and electrolytes are still high. We have to make sure Simone's weight, blood count, liver panel, kidney's, cultures, and lipid panel is functioning correctly. Her labs will determine if she has any diseases, liver damage, high cholesterol, and fatigue/bruising from low nutrition.

Okay, God, I need you to fix this situation.

Thanks for the prayer.

Hugs and Kisses.

Delon and Simone.

June 2, 2008

Hey y'all!

No, we aren't home yet. Simone was so disappointed. Hopefully, she'll be able to go home tomorrow. We are still trying to get her Potassium and kidney levels right. Of course, she wanted a day pass again.

Today, she had musical therapy. The teacher, this time, brought a piano for her to play on. Of course, Simone played it like she didn't miss a beat. She had a good day today even though she didn't leave the hospital.

Hugs and Kisses,

Delon.

June 3, 2008

Simone was discharged today!

Nine days short of six months. Thank you, Jesus! That same day, I finally was able to give her a bath. She surely enjoyed it. Can you imagine not feeling running water on your body for five months? She's still tube-fed—not eating through her mouth yet, but we know that is sure to follow.

June 8, 2008

On Sunday, Simone went to the church; yes, the church!

"The prayers of the righteousness avail much."

She enjoyed church, but some stares made her a little uncomfortable. That's okay; she still looks fabulous to me. Tomorrow she has labs again, so we are believing in God that those, too, will look good. Once you are discharged, labs are drawn twice a week just to see what the body is doing. Simone is still experiencing nausea, but we are working through it. Thanks again, for all the love and support.

"I NEVER WOULD HAVE MADE IT WITHOUT YOU GOD."

Since we are home now, I will update her website once a week.

We are still in the fight and winning, but SIMONE STILL NEEDS YOUR PRAYERS.

Hugs and Kisses,

Simone and Delon.

June 9, 2008

Well, family and friends, Simone is home! I am a week late, but we were trying to get used to the idea of being home!

July 10, 2008

Wow! We are still home!

I am so sorry for not writing sooner. Simone is doing wonderful. We still need to go to Jackson Memorial Hospital at least once a week. At first, we were required to go three times, but since she was doing so well, they decided to cut it down to once a week.

Simone celebrated her birthday last Saturday (7-5-2008). God is so, so, so good. So many family and friends came to support, and see the miracle, and to witness that consistent prayer does change things. What a ball she had! All we could do was to thank God for allowing Simone to see another day, and to celebrate her 15th birthday. Especially, since she just received her Multi Organ Transplant operation around Christmas. We weren't expecting her recovery to be so quick.

Once again, this is a daily walk. And as always, I could not have made through these last months without my family, friends, and your prayers.

I send so much love,

Delon and Simone Brewton.

April 13, 2009

Wow! We are still home! Yes, we are still home!

YOU SHOULD HAVE WHAT YOU SAY!!!

I am so sorry for not writing sooner. Simone is doing wonderful. We no longer have to go to Jackson Memorial Hospital every week. We also have graduated to having the dreadful scopes every three months. GOD IS SO GOOD!

Yesterday was RESURRECTION DAY! Last year we were in the hospital, but this time we were able to worship at church. Not only did Simone get to go to church, but she also was able to spend Spring break in South Carolina with her grandparents. She had a ball! All I can say is GOD IS AWESOME!

This should make you chuckle. All those who have followed Simone's story know that we struggled with Simone, and the water issue. Now the doctors want her to drink and, you guessed it, she does not want to drink. She isn't eating, and that's because she doesn't want to yet. But if we could get her to drink, she could get off the IV. Well, we aren't chuckling anymore. That was the old Simone.

The NEW Simone now eats at least one good meal and drinks 16 ounces of water a day. The best part is that she is no longer on the IV.

Simone has been dependent on the IV for 15 years, and finally, she drinks enough to sustain herself.

Once again, this is a daily walk, and as always, I could not have done any of this without my family, friends, and your prayers.

I send so much love,

Delon and Simone Brewton.

1 Comment

Simone Brewton: I LOVE YOU

Because everyone has those days and struggles while trying to get through life.

You're not alone.

Talks with Monie

April 26, 2016

My heart hurts, God. I was expecting you to turn this around. I can't quite figure out what was different about this situation. You always turned it around. I prayed and thought you were listening. Part of my guilt is feeling I didn't pray hard enough. Could I have made a difference? I witnessed something that no one should ever have to witness. Her organs failed. Why couldn't you bring them back to life lord? I saw her bleed out; why couldn't you stop the bleeding? I prayed and thought you were listening. My heart hurts! She was my everything. I remember Monie telling me she couldn't lose me. I cried and told her I needed her in my life and told her there would be no way I could make it through life without her. I'm just completely blown away.

I had faith and believed that everything would turn around. But did I really have the full faith I needed?

The day I lost my baby girl, was the hardest day of my life. I had no idea that this would be my life, our life. It should be the other way around. Parents should never have to see their child go.

I walked into the room and saw my pumpkin, Simone "lionheart" Brewton, lifeless. I stood there lifeless, and in disbelief, as well. I see my father sitting there hoping that she would come back, but we knew in that moment that it was over.

June 4, 2016

I saw Simone in my dream again. But this time she spoke to me. Today my friend Q is getting engaged. In my dream, Simone walked through the crowd while my best friend JB and I were sitting down. She said "Hey," with flowers in her hand. It freaked me out that I was able to hear her. Monie proceeded to sit next to me. I was able to see her; however, no one else could. I picked her up and put her on my lap. She whispered, "I will always have your back."

July 5, 2016

12:00 pm Today is your birthday, Monie. I cried my eyes out knowing I couldn't speak to you. Thought about calling your phone and leaving a voicemail. But I didn't. I knew it would've been too painful.

2:00 pm I put together a little party for you. We were LIT, lol! You loved bowling so that's what we did. Love was in the air. No pain, and no tears. Just love.

July 9, 2016

12:50 pm Today I listened to John Mayer Gravity. It reminded me of the time we went to Disney Quest when we were kids. You were upset because I picked the better CD. Miss you Monie.

1:23 am I performed at the world premiere of *Ghostbusters*. It was kinda awesome—just wish I could tell you about it. I also miss seeing your comments about me performing. I had taken it for granted.

3:23 am After coming home from the after-party, I cried in the bathroom for about an hour. Thinking about you, and how everything happened. I asked God why he would let it end this way. To be honest, I'm still confused by your death. I sent a text message to my grandmother. It said "I'm so sad, Grandma. Simone was just ok, and now she's gone!! My heart hurts. I'm pushing through my days, but it's been hard. I'm just destroyed inside. I'm lost without her." She called me, proceeded to tell me how good God is. Simone would've never wanted to be on this earth the way she was. She's complete in heaven now. I believe that, but I know you wanted to be here with us.

July 11, 2016

3:00 pm I spoke to dad. He recently started group counseling and personal therapy to help him with his grief. Dad misses you.

July 15, 2016

3:00 am Can't sleep. My thoughts won't allow me to rest. Keep thinking about the phone call I received from dad about you Monie.

July 18, 2015

2:55 pm Wanted to let you know that I got my friendship back. Who knew? Lol! You knew! You told me that we would become friends again, but I didn't see it. His girlfriend and I are cool as well. It's nice, actually. Hope you can hear me.

July 20, 2016

5:27 pm I saw an old friend at a showcase for choreographers, called Carnival. He passed me a few times and acted like I didn't exist. I hated that I went out of my way to speak. I also hate that I told him about you. There was no need for me to share that with him. It feels like I left a piece of you with him.

July 23, 2016

2:29 pm This week has been a bit emotional for me. I have these thoughts about death. It doesn't seem serious since I saw it firsthand. I've been feeling like I want to die just to be with you. I would never hurt myself, but I want to be closer to you. I received a DM from your page. It threw me off. I nearly almost cried in rehearsal. For a moment I thought it was you. Found out that it was Mom. I haven't been right since.

July 25, 2016

3:34 pm I started rehearsal today for a show with Christina Aguilera. You crossed my mind. I found myself reminiscing on our last Christmas together. Lawd, you gave me the biggest headache! You called me every morning asking me where I was. I made sure I was there every day by your side; Never once complained. Well, I'm leaving tomorrow afternoon for Batumi, Georgia. Miss you Monie.

July 26, 2016

4:45 pm Turbulence happened on the plane, and I found myself wanting to be with you. I was scared! But definitely thought about you in the moment. I'm drinking a lot more than I should. More than usual. Trying to slow down, but it helps me get through my day.

7:05 pm The hardest part is knowing that life still goes on.

July 30, 2016

11:45 am Hey, Simone! It's me again. I just messaged my old roommate Mykell, because I felt like I had no one else to turn to. I believe you met him once in Miami, when he was assisting Jaquel at a teaching convention for dance. What's crazy is that Mykell was in Cleveland, Ohio with Justin Bieber the same day you passed away. Who would've thought that he would've been in the same city. He rushed right over to our hotel to make sure our family was ok.

To Mykell:

"I feel so incomplete inside. I feel lost, and every day I want to cry. Sometimes I wish I could die to be with my sister. I do my best when I'm around people to keep it together. I don't trust pastors anymore, and I can't seem to get on the right track with God.»

Mykell— Sometimes we forget how much life matters. Pray about someone coming in your life. You can mentor in a way or aid. Lots of healing can take place in giving because giving from a pure place always requires more God and that fills us up more.

By default more God = more healing. When I've been the most broken, I give and it's not only reminding me that I'm bigger than my trials but that others still need me, that I can't give up, and that I'm not living in vain now that things have suffered.

Tasks:

1. Really be able to understand what tragedy is and how you see it. Is it more powerful than good and light to you? Do you believe that light wins or darkness? Do you believe death disqualifies all of the good that happens when we are alive or is it only as big as we allow it to impact our minds? Is it a real thing but NOT THE ONLY thing?

2. Keep sitting in God's presence, even if annoyed and have nothing to pray/say. This is also faith.

3. Find someone to sow into/mentor in some way. You'll birth something in you and them. You'll have more reasons to GO!

4. Don't try to fix your parent's hurt—it's bigger than you. Love them and pray for them but know that it's beyond you. You can't bear that weight, Bianca.

5. Continue creating. It doesn't replace what you've lost but it adds to what you have.

August 1, 2016

11:11 am We just finished our show with Christina Aguilera and now I'm flying home from Batumi, Georgia to see mom and Matt. Today was weird—not having you in the house. I slept with your favorite stuffed animal Pooh last night. You know I used to hate Pooh! Now I love him

August 6, 2016

12:00 am The hardest thing is creating new memories without you.

August 7, 2016

I miss the little things. Like you picking your lips to death, lol!

August 12, 2016

Sometimes I wish God would have taken me instead of you. I think the family would've handled it a little better.

August 22, 2016

10:45 pm You know I saw Mom and Matt. It was weird sleeping in the room without you. I should have had the time of my life, but I didn't. It taught me a lot about family, and how much they loved you. You were the piece that glued everyone together.

August 23, 2016

8:26 pm Life! Today I woke up to get ready for a movie I'm doing with Adam Sandler. His costar is Jennifer Hudson. She was extremely nice and welcoming. But all I kept thinking was: how is she able to be here right now with most of her family being gone? That situation was saddening, and every time I looked at her I was in awe. Her strength, man!

August 24, 2016

2:57 am I wanted to teach you how to love yourself, but I couldn't because I didn't know how to love myself. I miss you, Monie.

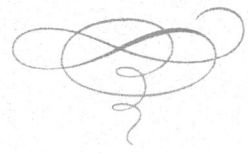

Selfishness

I felt ashamed, and it hurts to even write this. I was selfish for not letting my sister see who I really was. There were moments when I was trying to protect her because I didn't want her to be like me. Now, when I say I didn't want her to be like me I meant I didn't want her to see my insecurities, flaws, and to know that I'm really not perfect. In all honesty, I didn't want her doing what young adults would normally do. Even though Monie was 21, her mind was still playing catch-up from all the things she never really got to experience. I thought I was protecting her. I had moments where I pushed her feelings away; I just couldn't be bothered. Looking back on it now eats me up with guilt.

My sister looked up to me, and I feel like I let her down. She had moments where she would say she wasn't pretty enough, because of everything that's happened to her. I always reminded her of how beautiful and awesome she was. But in those moments, I didn't believe it about myself. Her hair fell out because of the radiation treatment, which I found out as an adult. Her teeth were built up with plaque, because of the medicine that she was taking. She was five feet tall, weighed 80 pounds and didn't have any breasts/ butt. It played on her insecurities. I was selfish with my feelings... And even when I expressed my insecurities, she couldn't relate, because she saw me as whole. I didn't look like her, so she never understood why I was complaining. I never saw her as being sick, because in my head she was normal. I thought you had it together Simone, but all you really wanted was my time. TIME! I'm not going to lie; I am still battling this one. There's guilt that I feel. From my perspective, I didn't do enough, and from Simone's eyes, I was the best sister EVER.

September 1, 2016

2:29 am Well, today is my birthday, and I'm still waiting to receive a phone call from you. I can hear your voice now "Happy Birthday big butt... Fly me out to California." You were filled with so much love. I miss that. I promise I'll make the best out of today, and I promise I won't cry, lol! I know you're calling me a big baby in Heaven right now.

September 2, 2016

1:47 am But what if there's no Heaven? What if after you die, that's it? Do you just expire? What if the Bible is a myth just to give people hope, and not real?

September 26, 2016

<u>2:21 am</u> Auntie Porcha sent a family video of us as kids: it's been sitting by the bed for a few days now. I don't think I can watch it. I'm not ready to see you, knowing that you aren't here.

<u>2:22 am</u> I took a break from writing because it shows me that you're actually GONE. It makes me think crazy thoughts.

November 6, 2016

<u>6:29 pm</u> I went to see *Doctor Strange*, and I must say it's a really good movie, Monie. I thought about all of those times you asked for me to take you to the movies, I'm missing that. But back to *Doctor Strange*. It had a lot of insight about life, and death. With life, sometimes we think that it's a privilege to be able to be alive. We forget that it's by God's grace that we are even alive. Everything that's handed to us is a little blessing from HIM showing us that we're on the right path.

November 13, 2016

<u>11:41am</u> YOU were my purpose.

November 29, 2016

<u>11:24 am</u> Simone, your home-schoolteacher called mom today to share her dream with her, which I'm sure you already knew. Once mom heard you showed up, she didn't want to hear it. However, I decided to take it upon myself to see what you were talking about.

(Ms. Jackson's dream) Simone said to Ms. Jackson "Now we can have girl-talk," and proceeded to sit on the bed. The layout was set up just like our old bedroom—two twin beds on each side of the room, TV down the middle with pink walls. Ms. Jackson was in disbelief. She questioned if that was really Monie. Simone said, "Are you done crying, I have a lot to say." Ms. Jackson says, "I feel like you weren't able to live your life," and Simone agreed. She remembered people standing over her and carrying her body out. Simone brought up the reason why she never came to anyone in their dreams. Seeing everyone hurting is making it hard for her to speak to us. I can't lie, hearing Ms. Jackson's dream made me mourn for you even more. I wish I could have these types of convos with you.

December 4, 2016

3:32 am You only have one life to live. So live it!

December 19, 2016–January 5, 2017

2:02 am It was a rough/awesome trip back home. What made it rough, was me. I could barely connect with dad. My guard was up most of the time, and Cookie tried her best, but I just wasn't feeling it. Also, I felt alone sleeping in the room without you. Depressed, and barely moved. I remember coming home late at night screaming out the window, calling your phone, asking for you to come and get me. Ha! You were over me. I remember lying beside you and checking to make sure you were breathing every night. I miss you Monie.

January 1, 2017

8:19 pm I watched a TV show called "The OA". I must say, it was beautifully written. There is such a powerful message in this series. We all are not perfect, but God gives us the chance to change our lives. We are all walking angels. Our duty is to spread love and light wherever we go. First time in a while that I've prayed and meant it. Last year showed me that my life is not my own.

January 26, 2017

12:56 pm These past few months I've been feeling a bit numb. I now realize that I danced for you, but now that you aren't here, I feel empty inside every time I move. Last night I had a dream that mom brought you to Chick-fil-A. I just held you tightly and cried my eyes out, knowing that I wouldn't have a long time with you. I miss you, Monie.

February 5, 2017

10:00 am Well, today is the big day! I'll be starting dance rehearsals for Justin Bieber's Purpose Tour. It's weird doing something new and not being able to tell you.

February 19, 2017

4:20 pm A quote from Mykell "Someone didn't see the day you're complaining about. Be grateful." Mykell gathered us for a group meeting/prayer. We all went one by one to talk about life, and to share what has been in our hearts. Everyone started to pour out. I was able to release a few things that I was feeling, such as committing suicide to be closer to you. You know, this experience has been great, but it has been really hard. It's almost been a year, and I still feel the pain.

March 7, 2017

7:54 pm Almost a year in, and you probably would've guessed I've found some peace. I still can't fully pray yet. I find myself in certain situations, calling on Him. I don't know if it's just by habit, or if it's genuine. Maybe everyone goes through the phases of coping. In my case, I recognize the triggers of my emotions. Like saying, "When my sister died…" or seeing pictures of her.

March 8, 2017

3:00 am My sister was a walking miracle!

March 10, 2017

4:30 pm I cried my eyes out before the show, and during the show, I made a point to release everything that I was feeling.

March 11, 2017

1:04 pm You've been on my heavy heart, Simone. To be on the road, and not be able to speak to you, or buy you little things from the different places I go, throws me for a loop. Spoke to mom, and she's still having a rough time. Still haven't spoken to dad though. It feels like we're growing apart.

March 15, 2017

3:10 pm I still can't seem to comprehend why you would take her. Why couldn't you heal her? And if you knew that you would take her, why would you drag out the process? I'm sure whatever answer I get, I will never quite understand. Where was the miracle in that? Now we are left in pain, and yes, I know it's a choice. But I can't seem to muster up the strength to get rid of this pain.

March 20, 2017

4:00 pm (Talks with God) How can I help my family, and myself if I don't press into him more? Also, you have been touring, but not showing anything for it. So it's time for me to do something different this time around ...

March 25, 2017

I am speaking on behalf of everyone who lost someone.

April 26, 2017

10:00 am Today makes a year that you've been gone and it started out rough. I cried my eyes out in disbelief that this is really my life without you. I am an emotional wreck. I also haven't spoken to Mom today. It's hard speaking to her, knowing that you could possibly come up in conversation. I don't want to revisit or reminisce about the past. Seems as though I want it on my own terms.

Love

Love is an action. There has to be some type of movement behind it. Growing up, I felt like I wasn't loved by my parents. Don't get me wrong, they loved me, but it was hard for me to see the action. They were so consumed with Simone, which they should've been. It made me feel like I was a bother at times. In some weird way, I knew my parents were dealing with a lot, and I sympathized with them. So maybe I wasn't a bother. It was just me trying to make their lives less stressful. For example, I would always say "You didn't have to give me anything for Christmas, because I know you're going through a lot with Simone." It sounds very small, but what seven-year-old kid would really want to give up Christmas?

There were a few years where I spent my winter breaks in the hospital with my sister. These were the moments I thought I needed to be sick to get some type of love or affection. My mom was the best, but I could feel the lack of affection from her. This is probably why I thought being sick was the way to get affection from people you loved. I was going off what I saw. I remember asking my grandmother why doesn't anyone love me. That stuck with me for many years. It got to the point where I started to dim my light because I thought I was too much. From elementary up into Monie's passing, I thought I knew how to love. But the reality was, I didn't understand love. It explained why I settled for less in my relationships. I was always people-pleasing to get some love or reaction. It wasn't healthy for me.

Her passing really made me dig deep and figure out what love was. I realized it was an action and choice. I was choosing to make myself uncomfortable so that I could finally love unconditionally. Sat in the house alone many nights to break down why I didn't have love for myself. Until one day I realized it stemmed from my childhood. I broke down every moment in my life. I'm glad I did that. I can finally say I am on the right path to loving myself. Me being uncomfortable was worth it.

June 16, 2017

Hearing the death of my friend's brother really struck a nerve in me. You see, Simone was sick, and we started to figure out that she didn't have long. But in this situation, it was so sudden. I couldn't comprehend how everyone else lived, and he didn't. He was so young and had so much life to live. But in that thoughtful moment, I found a little peace with my situation. Don't get me wrong, I'm still hurting for my friend, but the impact his brother had on the community and the world, spoke to me. He was able to fulfill his purpose. He graduated college with a doctor's degree, was able to work in a hospital as a doctor, changing lives, performed with *Boyz II Men*, and made it on

America's Got Talent. What a wonderful life he lived! I guess what I'm getting at is that we are the "vessels". It's our job to leave a huge impact on the world just like my sister, and Brandon.

June 25, 2017

<u>2:47 pm</u> Today I saw a massage therapist, but she was more of a spiritual healer. I walked towards her, and she said, "Oh, you need a massage." Didn't think anything of it so I began to lay down on the table. She adjusted my body, and I frowned because of the discomfort. She goes, "I don't want to hurt you more than you've been hurt. By now I'm already trying to figure out what she meant. She asks, "How old were you when you started beating down on yourself?" I break down thinking she may be speaking about Simone. I proceed to say older, and she goes, "You were younger," and now at this point, I knew what she meant. She said "You're putting on a role for everyone, and you are not allowing people to see who Bianca is. When are you going to forgive yourself? It's time to forgive yourself! You're beautiful, and you're more than enough."

July 5, 2017

<u>11:00 am</u> Happy Birthday to my beautiful sister, Monie! Even though you aren't physically here, I thank you for inspiring me each and every day. These past few months have been rough. Going in and out of depression because I couldn't physically speak to you about my accomplishments, tore me up. But now I'm starting to have a little bit more of peace of mind. Your death is actually giving me life. To be honest, I thought it was slowly killing me, but it's forcing me to find out who Bianca really is. I love you, Simone Sahara Brewton.

P. S your visits in my dreams bring me joy <3.

July 25, 2017

9:37 am I woke in terror after my dream about you. You walked in my rehearsal and sat down to observe. It threw me off because I knew you were gone. So I look at you like you're a ghost. You didn't say much, but when we started riding out, your face lit up. You looked heavier from afar, but when you came up close you actually looked your normal size. You hugged me and cried saying you didn't want to die. So this took me all the way down. But I was confused because you were already gone. It's almost like you didn't know you were. I woke from my sleep literally screaming at God, "Why would you do this?"

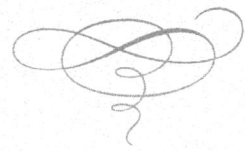

Relationships

I am afraid of being alone! I would say it's more of a fear—the fear of losing everyone; being stuck trying to figure out life. Part of that is not finding someone to love me for who I am. I've noticed that I put an expiration date on when I should fall in love/be married and when my focus should be on living out my purpose. Which I am! There are just these moments where I go into deep thoughts about life. Like, when my mom and dad pass away, who will walk me down the aisle? Or that my sister will never see my first child being born. It's funny because Simone always said I will have her children. We always went back and forth about that. Now, looking back, I would've done that for her. I would have done a lot of things differently.

Before her passing, my dad had a tumor that grew on his optic nerve, and after got prostate cancer—which he beat! If you want me to be honest, I'm scared. Since her passing, I've been doing my best to mend my relationships with my family and God. My love for God still existed. I was just pissed off for what he did. I could not wrap my head around how he brought her through every other time but not this time. You brought her through a five-organ transplant and could not bring her through this. I was confused, and still a little confused. She was my baby and was afraid to die. He knew that! I felt like she still had more life to her. I needed Simone! She was a puzzle piece to our lives. She held a special place in everyone's heart.

For the longest time, I was trying to figure out how to fill her shoes. I used to hear my family say Simone used to do this for us; you know she remembered everyone's birthday, etc. I realized I didn't know how to fit in with my own family. Now, I'm forced to learn how to just BE. This has been a slow journey building my relationships, but it's getting better.

August 1, 2017

<u>12:13 am</u> I'm Visiting my dad in Vegas today. He decided to take a break from Miami, and just live a little. I'm both excited and irritated. I guess I feel this way because part of me doesn't know what his emotional state is. I know I should be there for him regardless, but I can't seem to muster up the strength to get out of this dark zone to comfort him. It feels like there's a lot of pressure on me. I've never really had to give my parents my full attention because their full attention was on Monie. Now, there's no pity party here. It just seems easier to stay melancholy. Anyways, the trip took a left turn. I found myself more irritated, and ready to leave. My dad tried his best to make me happy, but I was being a jerk. We agreed to have a talk. He spoke to me with endearment and quickly expressed his pain. Apologizing for the lack of love, I felt I didn't get from him, or the family. But it's deeper

than that. Part of my issue is with the relationship between my sister, and my dad's fiancé. I believe Simone getting kicked out of the house drove her closer to being sick faster. You know there's still some mending to do, but I know by Christmas time, everything WILL be alright!

12:47 am Now, don't get it twisted. My father was the best dad. He made a lot of sacrifices for our family and will forever be my hero.

August 20, 2017

2:55 pm It's probably because God isn't the center of my life right now.

October 3, 2017

1:27 am I can't seem to stop my broken heart from hurting. I felt the same pain in my chest the day you passed. I needed to divert my attention, so I turned on the Tv and guessed what popped up, "Big hero 6." I remember us crying together when he lost his brother. We weren't expecting that movie to be so deep. It really took us down. I feel the guilt come over me again. I should've spent more time with you.

October 8, 2017

11:09 pm I found myself crying my eyes out because I can't seem to get a grip on my life. Seems like everything is spiraling down because I'm trying to do everything on my own. I've faced the fact that I don't know how to make proper decisions on my own, and relationships linger longer than they need to. Also, I looked up a psychiatrist to help me sort out my thoughts.

October 9, 2017

11:54 pm The weirdest thing: every time my heart feels broken, my right arm gets numb and starts to ache.

November 18, 2017

1:43 am I'm supposed to see my mom for Thanksgiving. The thought about seeing her and being there without Simone stirred up so many emotions. My mind immediately went straight to the first day of Simone's death. I've been trying to place a time when everything went crazy. You would think that by now I should have some bit of closure, or not be as emotional. But I must say, I am extremely excited to see her and can't wait to give her a big hug!

November 25, 2017

12:32 am Simone you were missed. I'm staying optimistic. Flying to Orlando to see the family was the best thing I could've ever done. I reconnected with old and new faces. If you were here, I would definitely get on your last nerve. I'm now realizing that I was the little sister when we were around family. I followed you everywhere, because I felt like I was out of place. So without you here, has forced me to open up. It has also forced me to reflect on all of our wonderful memories in Orlando as kids. We left our mark here. Disney Quest, Make-A-Wish foundation, Islands of Adventure etc. Those were good times Simone.

1:15 am I am renewing my mind. I will now move forward, and not focus on the bad. No more excuses. With that said, this week in Orlando was pretty awesome. My godmother came down to surprise me, and I must say she got me good. I became teary. I was even able to see my grandparents, and cousins whom I haven't seen in years. I found myself being comfortable around my family. There were a few times when I got depressed, which is normal. But I didn't let that stop me.

December 1, 2017

9:54 pm My days have been great so far! I am choosing to renew my mind and change my outlook on life. One day at a time.

December 6, 2017

7:33 pm This journey of living life without my sister has shown me a lot about myself. I'm realizing now as an adult that I associate love with being sick. That was the only way I thought I could receive attention as a child. There were times when I wished I could be in Simone's place. First, because it hurt me to see her go through life that way, and again because she got the love that I never felt was given to me. I was never jealous, not one bit; I just knew that was my place in life/purpose as a child: to not be in the way or be seen. During Christmas time, I would often tell my mother to not buy me Christmas presents. I knew it was hard on them, and again Simone was a priority. I was selfless. Some of these habits carried on into me being an adult. I now know that this way of thinking has to change!

Happiness

I found myself wondering how to find true happiness, not realizing that it was a choice. There were moments that I dwelled in sadness for most of my childhood, up until high school; she was in and out of the hospital. My emotions were all over the place not knowing when the time would actually come. Yeah, I was happy to be on tour. But I couldn't live it fully. The feeling of guilt would always haunt me. How could I truly be happy while my sister is dealing with this syndrome? I'm sure it seems like it could be easy, but it wasn't. I trusted God, but did I really? There was also the depression that lived in me, and I never understood that until later in my life. I needed to sit still. The more I stayed still, the more clarity I received. Now, the journey of trying to find true happiness was tough. It took a lot of uncomfortable moments to finally say, "It's enough." And as I get older, the concept of happiness starts to get clearer. I'm grateful for this journey of discovery.

December 12, 2017

1:01 am Monie, today is your second birthday. This is the day of your seven -organs transplant. I was in college, and I remember receiving a call saying you would have surgery later that day. I'm not going to lie; it was scary not knowing if you would make it out alive. The process was long. We went through a lot of complications, like one of your new organs failing right after the surgery. Your lips turned blue, and they had to stop your heart to try to fix the problem. It was tough seeing that as your sister. I stopped eating, started skipping school, and cried five days straight. I was mentally drained after witnessing that. If I must say, life is precious. Never take it for granted! With that said, I'm actually excited to see what my strength might look like next year.

December 25, 2017

12:47 am Today was surprisingly great. I woke up feeling like it was just another day instead of dwelling on Christmas. This holiday was her favorite. She constantly asked, Whatchu get me Big Butt?" and I would proceed to say nothing. When, in actuality, I had loads of stuff for her. I couldn't wait to shower her with gifts. Again, today was a great day. This trip so far has been refreshing, and better than the last.

December 26, 2017

6:11 pm Today has also been another great day! This time of the year hasn't been good to my mom and dad. They're struggling with keeping a smile on their face and if they do, it's just to hide what they feel inside. I told myself that I would be a lot more optimistic this time around just so I could have a different experience, and in order for that to happen, I needed to Speak to Cookie about Simone. That was the only way I could really move forward. I held on to a lot of hurt because of the type of relationship they had. Don't get me wrong, there were a lot of good times. I just felt like Simone and Cookie were both fighting for my dad's attention, and everyone being under one roof kind of spiraled the situation out of control—to the point where Simone had to leave my dad's house to stay with my grandmother. She was doing well there, but after some time her health started to go down. My mom remarried and moved to Georgia with her new husband. She was the one who kept everything in order. She made sure Simone stayed on top of her medicine and doctor appointments. Simone needed proper care. Looking back while writing this brings a tear to my eye, makes me feel like I could've done more as her sister. It's funny because I even thought about giving up my career to go to medical school to help my sister out. I wonder what life would've looked like if I had gone to medical school. Simone could've lived longer if we took proper care of her.

December 27- January 3, 2017- 2018

I'm beyond grateful for the experience and time I spent with my family. It felt like something shifted. This was the most time I've ever spent with my family on my dad's side. Usually, I come into town, see them on Christmas and New Year's, then I'm back in LA. But this time I made an effort. I thought about Simone many times but never slipped into my depression. The only time I felt sad was when I had an encounter with my uncle. You see, my father's brother and his children never came to Simone's funeral except for one. It tore my father up, and it still bothers him two years later.

My father believes that if he speaks to my uncle, he'll drop the word of God in him. To be frank, my dad isn't seeing eye-to-eye with God right now. I'm slowly finding my way around, but my dad is still holding on to it. I mean I can't blame him because he lost his daughter. But yeah, Dad just really wants my uncle to apologize for not being there, or to hear his real reasoning for not coming. For now, his answer is he couldn't get his money back for the trip he paid for a while ago.

May 25, 2018

4:24 am You know holding on to the pain makes you feel like they're still with you. Almost afraid to let go because you feel like you lose a piece of them.

August 7, 2018

2:57 pm I thank you, Simone, for loving me through all my imperfections. You were, and will always be, one of my teachers. I've learned so much about myself with you not being here. I've learned that I'm selfish, I've learned that I really don't know how to love, I've learned that I'm actually disconnected with the family. I've learned all these things without you being here. I miss you tremendously, but now I'm finally realizing that you aren't in any pain. Thank you for the light that you shined on me, and the world. You showed everyone what loving without boundaries looks like. Simone Sahara Brewton, you were the real MVP.

Bianca,

May this be the beginning of something great. Whatever you decide to do, Simone will be pleased.

Love,

Mom